NOTHING BUT TROUBLE

EXODUS 1; 5; 6

BY THE ISRAELITES

L IFE was terrible.

Long gone were the good old days when we Israelites lived in peace in Egypt, back when Joseph found favor with Pharaoh. Ahh...life was good back then.

But not anymore.

The new Pharaoh didn't remember Joseph and became worried that there were too many of us in Egypt. Instead of being our friend, he became a cruel, brutal tyrant.

The Egyptians forced our people to become slaves. Now mud, blood, and lots of tears filled our lives. We spent our long, grueling days making bricks out of sludge and straw under the hot Egyptian sun. With whips at our backs, they made us work faster.

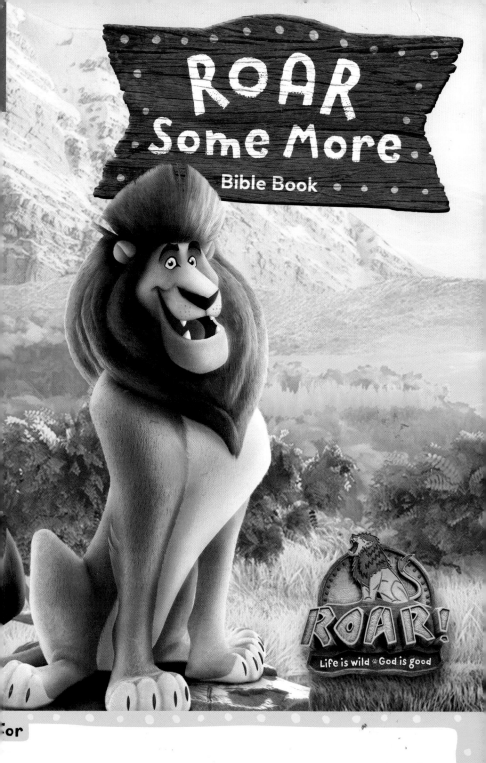

ROAR
Some More
Bible Book

ROAR!
Life is wild ~ God is good

For

Name

Loveland, Colorado
group.com/vbs

Group resources really work!

This Group resource incorporates our R.E.A.L. approach to ministry. It reinforces a growing friendshi
with Jesus, encourages long-term learning, and results in life transformation, because it's:

Relational—Learner-to-learner interaction enhances learning an
builds Christian friendships.

Experiential—What learners experience through discussion an
action sticks with them up to 9 times longer than what they simpl
hear or read.

Applicable—The aim of Christian education is to equip learners t
be both hearers and doers of God's Word.

Learner-based—Learners understand and retain more when th
learning process takes into consideration how they learn best.

Roar Some More Bible Book

Copyright © 2019 Group Publishing, Inc./ 0000 0001 0362 4853

Visit our websites:
group.com
group.com/Roar

We're wild about this VBS team:
Laura-Baldwin-Stout, Jody Brolsma, Stephen Caine, Shelly Dillon,
Lyndsay Gerwing, Elisa Hansen, Jan Kershner, Laycie McClain,
Michael Paustian, Kelsey Perry, Mike Porter, Joani Schultz, Patty
Smith, Rodney Stewart, and Gabriele Woolever.

Scripture quotations are taken from the Holy Bible, New Living
Translation, copyright © 1996, 2004, 2015 by Tyndale House
Foundation. Used by permission of Tyndale House Publishers, Inc.,
Carol Stream, Illinois 60188. All rights reserved.

ISBN 978-1-4707-5646-8

Printed in the USA. 001 USA 0918

10 9 8 7 6 5 4 3 2 1   21   20   19   18

When life is unfair...God is good!

"The Lord is good, a strong refuge when trouble comes."
(Nahum 1:7)

Meet Macko

One Cool Continent!

Africa isn't just elephants and giraffes. Which of these places would *you* be most excited to check out, and why?

Pyramids of Giza

So big you can see them from space!

Surfing

Some of the wildest waves in the world.

Gorillas

They're endangered, so spotting them is a big deal.

Victoria Falls

One of the world's *hugest* waterfalls.

Penguins

It's true!

2

But God saw our suffering. God decided now was the time to set his people free. God hatched a plan for Moses to tell Pharaoh to let God's people go.

Moses made up all kinds of excuses for God to find someone else, but God wanted *him* to be our leader.

So Moses teamed up with his brother, Aaron, and they marched straight to Pharaoh's palace.

MOSES and Aaron told Pharaoh everything God had said: "God says to let his people be free."

But Pharaoh just got mad.

"You're all just a bunch of lazy, good-for-nothing slackers!" Pharaoh yelled. "Get back to work!"

Not only did Pharaoh *not* let the Israelites go, but he made our lives even worse. He ordered the slave bosses to beat us even harder with whips and forced us to make even *more* bricks...without any straw. What?!

We were more miserable than ever.

But God wasn't done.

God said, "I am the Lord. I will rescue you from your slavery. I will bring you into the land I swore to give you long ago. I am the Lord!"

The excitement was about to begin.

Sometimes it can be hard to remember all the good things God has promised. It's like wondering if the sun is still up there behind the clouds after it's been raining for days.

Whether you can see the sun or not, it's there.

It's the same with God. If there's one thing that's always true, it's that God is good.

God is *always* good. No matter how unfair life gets, God's goodness never goes away. God is so, so good. And he knows the big picture.

When was a time you were treated unfairly? Did something bad happen to you that you didn't deserve? Whatever happened, you can trust that God was with you, just like he was with us. God loves you and cares about what happens to you. Take a moment every day to thank God for at least one good thing in your life.

―THE ISRAELITES―

When life is scary...God is good!

> "Even when I walk through the darkest valley, I will not be afraid, for you are close beside me."
> (Psalm 23:4)

Meet Hooper

Use in Imagination Station

Cut out these fears to feed to your Hungry Hoopoe. On the blank one, fill in something *you're* afraid of.

Storms

The dark

Bugs

Snakes

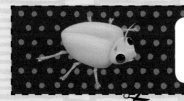

WHEN FEAR ~IS NEAR~

EXODUS 7:14–12:32

BY
ISRAELITE KIDS

W E used to like frogs. They're so cute!

But after you've seen a gazillion frogs piled up to your knees everywhere you go, they're just not as fun as they used to be.

It started when Moses told Pharaoh to let our people go free. But Pharaoh wouldn't listen.

So God showed Pharaoh who was boss. God sent Moses and his brother, Aaron, to meet Pharaoh on the bank of the Nile River. Just as God told him to do, Aaron hit the river with his wooden stick—SMACK!—and the water turned into blood!

The fish in the river died and floated to the top. All the water in Egypt—even the water in pots and bowls—turned to blood. Yuck! It smelled so gross!

But did Pharaoh change his mind? Nope. Pharaoh held his nose, then shrugged his shoulders and went back to his palace.

God sent Moses and Aaron to try again. This time when Pharaoh refused, God sent bajillions of frogs. Their croaks filled our ears all day long. They hopped everywhere—even in Pharaoh's palace and bed. They jumped into the houses of the Egyptians, into their ovens, and into their dishes. Frogs were everywhere!

Still, Pharaoh didn't listen. He would NOT let us go.

NINE times God sent Moses and Aaron to tell Pharaoh to set the Israelites free. Each time Pharaoh said no, God sent another plague. And each plague was worse than the last.

- Gnats filled the skies.
- Swarms of flies were everywhere.
- Egyptians' farm animals died.
- The people got sores that hurt to touch.
- Hail and lightning wrecked their stuff.
- Locusts ate their fields bare.
- Darkness fell over Egypt for three days.

Pharaoh's people were crushed. But stubborn Pharaoh wouldn't budge. "NO!" he said again and again and again.

Finally, God had enough. God sent a tenth and final plague—the most frightening one of all. Every firstborn Egyptian son, even Pharaoh's oldest boy, would die.

But God saved the Israelites—every one of us. And then Pharaoh, through his anger and tears, *finally* let us go.

We were free!

And God was good.

Have you ever been scared? Of course you have! Everyone feels afraid sometimes. And there are a lot of scary things in the world, like storms and bugs and death and darkness.

But God is good! And God is bigger than ANYTHING that frightens you. God promises to stay close beside you, no matter where you go.

Whenever you feel fear, stop and pray. Ask God to protect you.

Take five seconds to think about one thing that scares you. Yikes! It's no fun to focus on our fears. Now take 30 seconds to think about how much God loves you and takes care of you. Doesn't that feel better? Remember, God is ALWAYS good, and he ALWAYS loves you.

ISRAELITE KIDS

Day 3

When life changes...God is good!

"Give thanks to the Lord, for he is good! His faithful love endures forever."
(Psalm 106:1)

Use one of these these coupons with your Presto Chango!

God is good to ME!

God is always good!

THE WINDS OF CHANGE

EXODUS 14–17

BY
MIRIAM

FREEDOM!

We packed up our things, raised our fists in the air, and hurried straight out of Egypt. With my brother Moses as our faithful hero, and God, our mighty king, we began a fresh start. We had been slaves, but now we were free!
But with our freedom came lots of changes.

Instead of homes, kitchens, and beds, we moved, day after day, through a stark land of rocks and sand.

We couldn't help wondering if we'd made the right choice. We'd barely escaped from Pharaoh when we found ourselves trapped—the massive Red Sea in front of us and Pharaoh's army right behind us. Yikes!

But God rescued us yet again! Moses stretched out his hand, the winds roared, and the sea split in two. We raced across on dry land, and when we were safe on the other side, God filled the sea back up, swallowing Pharaoh's army.

God is good! I picked up my tambourine, started dancing, and led the people in a song of victory.

Now on to the Promised Land! But the journey got tough.

THERE wasn't much to eat or drink in that hot, dry wasteland. It didn't take long for our people to start complaining. They grumbled and mumbled and moaned to Moses.

"What are we going to drink?" they whined.

We traveled for three days without finding any water. Three whole days! And when we came to the oasis at Marah, the water was too bitter to drink.

These were NOT the changes we were hoping for.

Yet God was good!

God told Moses to toss a piece of wood into the water, and it instantly became good and fresh. We finally had plenty to drink.

We traveled on, and the complaining continued.

"We're going to starve out here in the wilderness!"

"We should have stayed in Egypt. We had plenty of food there!"

But God showed his goodness. Every evening he sent quails for us to roast and eat. And every morning he covered the ground with a strange sort of bread.

"What is it?" the people asked when they saw it.

"Bread from heaven," Moses said.

It tasted like honey wafers. Not bad! We called it *manna*.

So that's how we ate every day. At night God delivered quails for us to eat, and every morning the manna appeared on the ground. We gathered just enough for our families to eat for the day, and we never went hungry again.

God is so good!

Those weren't easy times for us Israelites. Traveling across the desert was a hard way to live. Life was changing. But God planned a better future for us in the Promised Land.

Sometimes God lets changes happen because he knows there's something better ahead of us. It's not always fun or easy, but it's always worth it. Staying close to God through life's changes is always the best choice we can make.

That's why God is so good. God wants the best for us. We can face any change that comes our way because God's goodness never ends.

What's a change you've gone through? Maybe you moved to a new house or a new town. Maybe you changed schools. Maybe you got a new brother or sister. Take a moment to stop and thank God for the good things that happen when your life changes.

MIRIAM

Day 9

When life is sad... God is good!

"The Lord is close to the brokenhearted." (Psalm 34:18)

Meet Zion

25

Make someone smile!

Use this fun Mad Lib to turn sad to happy!

It was a _____ day in Africa. Serengeti Eddy was lost.
[adjective]

And that made him sad. "I should have packed a _____
[noun]

for my trip," said Eddy. He _____ through the tall
[verb-past tense]

grass, looking for _____. But all he saw was a
[relative's name]

_____ and a _____. Then he saw a lion!
[noun] [noun]

Eddy was so _____ that he _____. Then he
[emotion] [verb-past tense]

_____ in a watering hole. But he couldn't swim. So
[verb-past tense]

sad! So Eddy _____ as fast as he could. He ran
[verb-past tense]

right into a _____ rhino! The rhino gave him a ride
[color]

back to _____. Eddy wasn't sad anymore! He was so
[place]

happy that he _____! He'll never get lost again!
[verb-past tense]

26

The Saddest Day of Our Lives

JOHN 16–21

BY JESUS' FRIENDS

HAVE you heard the most amazing story of all time? Listen close because we're going to tell you what happened to the greatest person who ever lived, died...and lived again.

His name is Jesus, and we were his disciples—his closest friends. We were there when Jesus walked on water and healed people. We were there when Jesus showed love to people who'd never been loved before.

We were there at his last meal, when Jesus said one of his disciples—one of *us!*—was going to betray him. He also said he wasn't going to be around much longer. He said we'd be sad but that when he came back, we'd be filled with so much joy that no one could ever take it away from us.

And just like Jesus said, one of the disciples *did* betray him. Judas told the Roman soldiers that Jesus would be in a certain garden praying. We were there when the Roman soldiers surrounded him with weapons and torches, arrested him, and took him away.

We couldn't believe what happened. Jesus loved everyone! He had never done anything wrong. Not once! Why were they treating him like a criminal?

Our hearts ached with sadness. But things only got worse.

They mocked Jesus. They hurt him. Then they nailed him to a big wooden cross.

Jesus didn't deserve to suffer like that. We'd done bad things our whole lives. *We* should've been up on that cross. But Jesus took our place.

And then Jesus died.

WE'D never been sadder in our lives.

They wrapped Jesus' body in cloths and laid him in a stone tomb. For three dark days, we stayed hidden. We were afraid we'd be arrested too. We felt lost and empty.

Then three days after Jesus died, on Sunday morning, something amazing happened.

Early in the morning, a few of us went to the tomb. We found that the heavy stone at the entrance had been rolled away. And the tomb was empty—Jesus wasn't there! Two angels suddenly appeared, wearing dazzling robes. They said, "Why are you looking among the dead for someone who is alive? He isn't here! He is risen from the dead!"

It was true! Jesus was alive! And he's alive today!

Jesus took the punishment for all our sins. Without Jesus, we'd have to carry the weight of our dirty, heavy sins. Our hearts would be hardened. We'd be separated from God. But because Jesus loves us so much, he took the punishment for our sins so we don't have to carry them anymore. We can be forgiven and be close to God.

God is so, so, so, so GOOD!

When you're sad, you feel drained, like an orange with all its juice squeezed out. That's how we felt when Jesus was killed. Empty.

But God is good. God fills our emptiness with something wonderful. His goodness pours into our broken, hollow spaces and fills us with his never-ending love. God filled our empty lives with Jesus, and he can do that for you, too.

Life can be sad. But no matter how gloomy things get, God is always good. He has something good in mind for you.

Do you know someone who's sad? YOU can be just the person God uses to fill that person with his love. Find someone who could use a refill today. Give that person a hug, say "I love you," or simply encourage the person with a kind word.

⟡ JESUS' ⟡ FRIENDS

When life is good...
God is good!

"Remember the Lord, who is great and glorious." (Nehemiah 4:14)

Meet Savanna

Remember the good times we had at Roar VBS!

As Good as It Gets

JOSHUA 3–4

BY

JOSHUA

WHAT a good day!

We'd been stuck in the desert for forty years. That's a long, long time. So much had happened since our people had left Egypt. God had given us his Ten Commandments. Moses had died. And we'd eaten more quail and manna than you could possibly imagine. And now *I* was the new leader of God's people.

All that wandering left me wondering: Would the people of Israel finally love and trust God?

We had every reason to be hopeful. God brought us up to the very edge of Canaan—the Promised Land—the land he had promised our ancestors long ago. All we had to do was cross the Jordan River, and we'd finally set foot in the country we could call home. One small problem— it was harvest season and the river was overflowing its banks. We couldn't get across!

But wait—hadn't the Israelites been in a similar situation forty years ago at the Red Sea? God had parted the water then, and he was about to do it again.

God told us exactly what to do. The priests carried the Ark of the Covenant to the edge of the Jordan River. As soon as the priests' feet touched the water, God caused the water to stop flowing in both directions. The priests carried the Ark into the middle of the river on dry ground. Then they held it there while all the Israelites walked across.

You should have seen the smiles on everyone's faces! We had finally made it!

WE never wanted to forget this. And since I know we're pretty good at forgetting, we needed to do something. We needed to celebrate and thank God for keeping his promise.

While the priests held up the Ark of the Covenant in the river, twelve men—one from each tribe of Israel—each picked up a large stone from the riverbed and carried it to the place where we camped for the night.

We piled the stones into a memorial. It was a special reminder of God's power and his promise. God parted the Jordan River at the end of our journey, just like he parted the Red Sea at the beginning of our journey, keeping us safe and moving us forward. God kept his promise of bringing his people into the Promised Land, a place where we could raise our families and worship God in freedom.

Our memorial stood as a rock-solid reminder that GOD IS GOOD. Yes, God is very good.

What's *your* stone?

We placed our stones on the memorial as a way to remember the good things God had done for us. God parted the Jordan River so we could walk across safely. Every time we looked at the stones, we could remember how much God loves us.

What good things has God done for you? You have family and friends who love you, yes? How has God provided you with food, a home, and things to enjoy? When was a time God kept you safe? What talents and skills has God given you?

There are so many good things God has done for you, and it's important to take time to remember those good things. Find one thing around your bedroom that reminds you of how much God loves you. Make it your "stone"—your memorial of how good God really is.

.⊪ JOSHUA ⊩.

Play Buddy Trek

(Turn the page for a bonus Buddy board game!) ▶ ▶ ▶

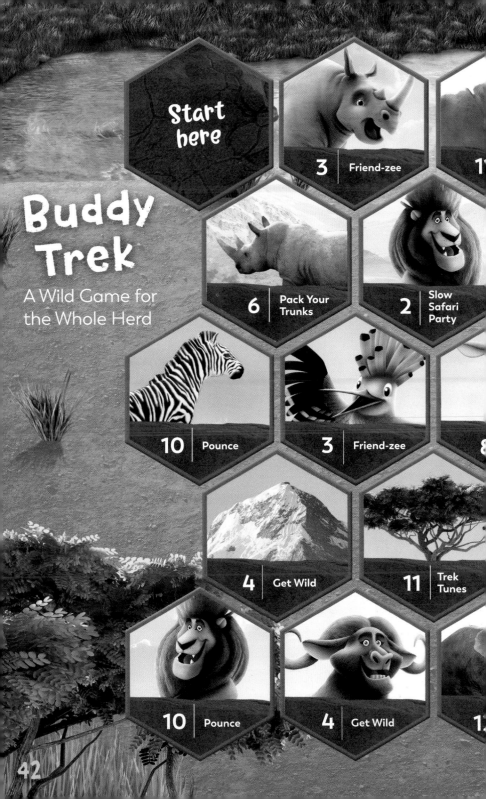

k
nes

9 | Join the Pack

5 | Ha-Ha-Hyena

12 | Gross Grazing

7 | Cool Cats

ampede

2 | Slow Safari Party

6 | Pack Your Trunks

9 | Join the Pack

7 | Cool Cats

ross
razing

5 | Ha-Ha-Hyena

8 | Stampede

God is good!

Take your Buddies to the watering hole to play!